Fla...

CUl...

RECIPES

Compiled by Julia Skinner

THE FRANCIS FRITH COLLECTION

www.francisfrith.com

First published in the United Kingdom in 2012 by The Francis Frith Collection®

This edition published exclusively for Bradwell Books in 2012
For trade enquiries see: www.bradwellbooks.com or tel: 0800 834 920
ISBN 978-1-84589-693-5

British Library Cataloguing in Publication Data

Flavours of ... Cumbria - Recipes
Compiled by Julia Skinner

The Francis Frith Collection
Oakley Business Park,
Wylye Road, Dinton,
Wiltshire SP3 5EU
Tel: +44 (0) 1722 716 376
Email: info@francisfrith.co.uk
www.francisfrith.com

Printed and bound in Malaysia
Contains material sourced from responsibly managed forests

Front Cover: **ULVERSTON, KING STREET 1912** 64396p
Frontispiece: **DERWENT WATER, LOOKING TOWARDS BARROW HOUSE c1900** D26301
Contents: **CARLISLE, THE MARKET PLACE 1937** C211001

The colour-tinting is for illustrative purposes only, and is not intended to be historically accurate

AS WITH ANY HISTORICAL DATABASE, THE FRANCIS FRITH ARCHIVE IS CONSTANTLY BEING
CORRECTED AND IMPROVED, AND THE PUBLISHERS WOULD WELCOME INFORMATION ON
OMISSIONS OR INACCURACIES

CONTENTS

RECIPES

MUTTON BROTH

Mutton is the meat of a fully grown sheep. It was once staple fare throughout the country, and Cumbria was famous for the well-flavoured mutton of the Herdwick sheep that graze the Lakeland hills. Mutton is now making a comeback, but if it proves hard to find you can use scrag end of lamb instead for this recipe, which makes a good hearty soup for cold winter days.

    450g/1 lb scrag end of mutton, or lamb
    2 carrots
    1 medium turnip
    1 onion
    25g/1oz pearl barley
    Salt and pepper
    A sprig of fresh parsley
    1.75 litres/3 pints of water

Cut the meat into small pieces and place it in a large saucepan with the water. Peel the turnip and onion, and chop the carrot, turnip and onion into small pieces. Put the chopped vegetables and the pearl barley into the saucepan with the meat, and season to taste with salt and pepper. Bring to the boil, then reduce the heat, cover the pan and leave to simmer gently for 2 hours. Just before serving, remove any bones from the broth. Finely chop the parsley and add to the broth, then serve piping hot, with hunks of brown bread.

ESKDALE GREEN, BOW FELL 1932 E194048

CREAM OF LEEK SOUP

Annual shows are held in a number of places in Cumbria where leek-growers win prizes for their giant vegetables, such as Aspatria, near Maryport, and Alston, a former lead-mining town south-east of Carlisle in the Cumbrian Pennines. However, for cooking purposes it is best to use smaller leeks!

25g/1oz butter
700g/1½ lbs leeks, trimmed, sliced and washed
2 onions, peeled and finely chopped
2 sticks of celery, chopped into small pieces
1.2 litres/2 pints chicken or vegetable stock
Salt and pepper
150ml/ ¼ pint/5 fl oz double cream
1 tablespoonful snipped chives, to garnish

Melt the butter in a large pan, add the leeks, onions and celery and cook for 10 minutes, until softened but not browned. Add the stock, season to taste and bring to the boil. Reduce the heat, cover the pan and simmer for about 30 minutes, until the vegetables are tender. Allow to cool slightly, then process in a blender or liquidizer until smooth and return to the pan. When ready to serve, add the cream and heat through, but do not allow the soup to boil. Serve with a garnish of chopped chives on each helping.

ALSTON, MARKET SQUARE
1952 A290014

MORECAMBE BAY

The shoreline of Morecambe Bay runs north from Fleetwood in Lancashire then follows the coast of southern Cumbria around the Cartmel and Furness peninsulas. The main Cumbrian settlements around the bay are Arnside, Grange-over-Sands, Ulverston and Barrow-in-Furness, on the south-western tip of the Furness peninsula, which sprang from a tiny hamlet in the 19th century to become the country's largest producer of iron and steel. Protected by the enclosing reef of the Isle of Walney, Barrow also flourished as a major shipbuilding centre in the 19th and early 20th centuries. In this photograph from 1912, shipbuilders swarm across Walney Bridge from the dockyards at the end of a working day. A crane at Vickers dockyard can be seen in the distant background on the right of this view.

BARROW-IN-FURNESS, WALNEY BRIDGE 1912 64407

RECIPE

COCKLE SOUP

Cockles have been harvested from the rich cockle beds in the sands all around Morecambe Bay for centuries, and this is still an important local industry. Cockles are often sold ready cooked and out of their shells, to be eaten cold, splashed with vinegar, with brown bread and butter. Fresh cockles bought in their shells can also be used to make this tasty soup, full of the flavour of the sea.

> 1.2 litres/2 pints measure (about 50) fresh cockles in the shells
> 25g/1oz butter
> 25g/1oz plain flour
> 300ml/ ½ pint milk
> 2 sticks of celery, very finely chopped
> Salt and pepper
> 2 tablespoonfuls finely chopped fresh parsley

Put the cockles in a bowl of lightly salted water for about one hour, to remove the sand. Scrub the shells well, then put them in a large pan and cover with well-salted water. Bring the water gently to the boil, shaking the pan from time to time, and cook the cockles until they have just opened – don't cook them any longer, as this will toughen them. Discard any cockles that do not open. Leave to cool, then strain the cockles, reserving the cooking liquid. Remove the cockles from their shells with the point of a sharp knife. Melt the butter in a pan, stir in the flour, then gradually mix in 600ml (1 pint) of the cockle water and the milk whilst bringing the mixture to the boil, stirring continually, until it has thickened and formed a smooth consistency. Add the celery, reduce the heat and simmer for 30 minutes, then add the shelled cockles, most of the chopped parsley and salt and pepper to taste. Cook for a few minutes longer before serving, garnished with the reserved chopped parsley.

RECIPE

POTTED SHRIMPS

Morecambe Bay is also famous for particularly delicious brown shrimps that are found here, and potted shrimps are a local delicacy. A centre of both cockle and shrimp fishing in the Cumbrian part of the Bay is Flookburgh, a charming village on the Cartmel peninsula. Local fishermen venture out across the sands as the tide ebbs, gathering the shrimps using specially adapted tractors with long nets hung from outriggers. If you can't get fresh Morecambe Bay brown shrimps for this recipe, you can use 350g/ ¾ lb shop-bought frozen shrimps or prawns instead, thoroughly defrosted before use.

> 225g/8oz unsalted butter
> 1 tablespoonful water
> 1 teaspoonful ground mace
> 2 good pinches cayenne pepper
> Freshly grated nutmeg, a generous helping
> 450g/1 lb fresh shrimps (or prawns – see above)
> Salt

Melt the butter slowly in a small pan with the water, taking care not to let it brown. Pour the melted butter into a bowl to cool, and place in the fridge and leave until the butter has hardened. Remove the solid (clarified) butter and discard the liquid that has settled beneath it. Melt 115g/4oz of the clarified butter in a large saucepan with the spices, then add the shrimps or prawns, lower the heat right down and let them steep in the hot butter for 10 minutes – they must not cook in the heat or they will become tough. Taste for seasoning and add salt, if needed. Pour the shrimps or prawns with the butter into small pots, and leave until the butter has set. Melt the remaining clarified butter and pour enough over the top of each pot to form a seal. Allow to cool, then keep in the fridge until needed. Take out of the fridge for about half an hour before serving, to allow the chill to go off, which gives the spiced butter more flavour. Serve with hot toast or crusty bread.

FLOOKBURGH, THE VILLAGE STREET 1906 56113x

RECIPE

STUFFED HERRINGS WITH MUSTARD SAUCE

Fishing boats still work out of harbours along the Cumbrian coast such as Workington, Maryport and Whitehaven, where a herring fishing industry was developed by Sir James Lowther in the 18th century. This recipe from Cumbria serves stuffed herrings with a tangy mustard sauce that cuts through the oiliness of the fish. Mackerel is also very good served this way. Serves 4.

<u>For the stuffed herrings:</u>
4 large herrings
3 heaped tablespoonfuls
  fresh white breadcrumbs
1 heaped dessertspoonful
  finely chopped parsley
1 teaspoonful lemon juice
Grated rind of half a lemon
Salt and black pepper
Oil for frying
25g/1oz butter

<u>For the mustard sauce</u>
40g/1½ oz butter
25g/1oz plain flour
450ml/ ¾ pint milk
Salt and black pepper
1 level tablespoonful dry
  mustard powder
1 tablespoonful white wine
  vinegar
1 level teaspoonful caster
  sugar

Remove the heads from the herrings, clean, gut and bone them. Wash the fish and pat them thoroughly dry. Put the breadcrumbs, parsley, lemon juice and lemon rind in a bowl, and season lightly with salt and freshly ground black pepper. Melt the butter and stir into the breadcrumbs to bind the mixture, which should be moist, but still crumbly. Stuff the herrings with the mixture, and if necessary secure them with wooden cocktail sticks. Slash the skin of each herring crossways two or three times on each side, brush the fish with oil and wrap each in foil. Put the fish in a well-buttered deep baking dish. Cover with lightly buttered greaseproof paper and bake in the centre of a pre-heated oven at 200°C/400°F/Gas Mark 6 for 35-40 minutes.

For the mustard sauce, melt 25g/1oz of the butter in a pan; stir in the flour and cook for 1 minute. Gradually stir in the milk, beating well until the sauce is quite smooth. Bring to the boil and simmer for 2-3 minutes, then season to taste with salt and pepper. Blend the mustard powder with the vinegar, stir into the sauce and add the sugar. Check the seasoning and stir in the remaining butter.

Transfer the baked herrings to a hot serving dish and serve the mustard sauce separately.

WHITEHAVEN, THE HARBOUR AND TOWN 1950 W313014

9

BASSENTHWAITE AND SKIDDAW c1880 B684301

RECIPE

SALMON WITH CUCUMBER AND DILL SAUCE

Salmon from the River Kent was once so plentiful in the Kendal area that a local school's rule book stipulated that the schoolboys should not be 'compelled to dine on salmon or fish in general more than 3 days a week'. This way of serving cold salmon with a cucumber sauce dates from Victorian times and is an ideal dish for summer days. This recipe uses soured cream – look for it in the cream section of supermarkets. If soured cream is hard to find you can use natural yogurt instead, which makes a tangier sauce.

> 1 whole salmon, about 1.8kg/4 lbs in weight, gutted and scaled
> 25g/1oz butter, melted
> 3 parsley or thyme sprigs
> Half a lemon, cut into slices
> 1 large cucumber
> Salt and pepper
> 15g/ ½ oz extra butter for the sauce
> 300ml/ ½ pint soured cream or yogurt
> 3 dessertspoonfuls of finely chopped fresh dill

Pre-heat the oven to 220°C/425°F/Gas Mark 7. Season the salmon and brush it inside and out with melted butter. Place the herbs and lemon slices in the cavity. Wrap the salmon in foil, folding the edges together securely. Bake in the pre-heated oven for 15 minutes. Take the fish out of the oven and leave in the foil for 1 hour, then remove the skin.

Meanwhile, peel the cucumber, cut it in half lengthways and scoop out the seeds. Cut the cucumber into small cubes, place them in a colander and sprinkle lightly with salt. Leave for 30 minutes to allow the superfluous liquid to drain, then rinse well and pat dry with kitchen paper. Heat the extra butter in a saucepan, add the cucumber and cook for 10-15 minutes, until it is translucent and soft. Leave to cool for a few minutes then push it through a sieve or process it in a blender or liquidizer. When ready to serve, mix the cucumber purée with the soured cream or yogurt and chopped dill, season to taste and serve immediately with the cold salmon.

HAAF-NETTING

The Vikings settled in parts of Cumbria over a thousand years or so ago, and that Norse heritage is recalled in many local place names, as well as words still in everyday speech in the region – such as 'beck' for a stream, 'fell' for a mountain, 'dale' for a valley and 'thwaite' for a clearing in a wood or forest. The Vikings introduced 'haaf-netting' to the Solway coast of northern Cumbria, and this ancient method of shallow water fishing still takes place in the Solway Firth and the estuary of the River Eden, particularly for salmon and sea trout, although nowadays haaf-netting is strictly licensed by the Environment Agency to protect fish stocks. The 'haaf' is a large fishing net mounted on a rectangular wooden frame 18 feet long by 5 feet high, supported by three legs. The haaf-netter wades out to stand chest-deep in the water and places the frame across the current, facing either the incoming or outgoing tides, then stands behind the net, holding the central upright. The net streams out in the water and when a fish swims into it the legs of the frame are allowed to float to the surface, thereby trapping the fish. The equipment and techniques have changed very little since Viking times, and haaf-net fishing has been described as a unique example of living archaeology.

BURGH BY SANDS, TOWARDS SCOTLAND ACROSS THE SOLWAY FIRTH c1950   B709010

RECIPE

BAKED TROUT

The Troutbeck Valley of the Lake District takes its name from the stream that flows through the valley, whose name means exactly that – 'the trout stream'. Serves 4.

> 4 trout, gutted, cleaned and washed
> 4 sprigs of fresh parsley, finely chopped
> 4 sprigs of lemon thyme, finely chopped
> 75g/3oz softened butter
> Salt and pepper
> 150ml/ ¼ pint white wine

Pre-heat the oven to 180°C/350°F/Gas Mark 4. Mix the chopped herbs into 50g (2oz) of the butter. Divide the herb butter into four pieces, and put one piece in the cavity of each fish. Place the fish closely together in an ovenproof serving dish, laying them alternately head to tail to fit into the dish, and season to taste. Pour the wine over the fish. Cover with foil, and bake in the pre-heated oven for 20-25 minutes, until the fish are tender. When the fish are cooked, dot them with the remaining butter, cut into small pieces, then return to the oven, uncovered, and bake for a further 10 minutes.

TROUBECK, THE VALLEY c1880 12523

WINDERMERE, A KEEN CONTEST c1800 W109301

WINDERMERE CHAR

A rare freshwater fish that is found in the deep, cold waters of Lake Windermere in Cumbria is the char. This is a relative of Arctic char, and is believed to be a very old species of fish that was left behind in the inland lake at the end of the last Ice Age, as the glaciers melted. Char has a delicately-flavoured flesh with a pinkish tinge. It is caught using a distinctive traditional technique using two long wooden poles that arch away gracefully from the fishing boat, from which long fishing lines are suspended, weighted with metal spinners; this allows fishermen to suspend the bait at great depth, as the char can feed at anything up to 90 feet down. Potted char was very popular as a breakfast dish in the 17th, 18th and 19th centuries, when it was served in special 'char dishes' made of white china decorated with pictures of the fish, which are collectors' items today.

BORROWDALE, CASTLE CRAG c1865 2774

Huge numbers of sheep are reared on the hill farms and moorlands of Cumbria, where hardy breeds such as the Herdwick, Swaledale (seen in this photograph) and Rough Fell can withstand the cold winds and bitter winters. Shepherds' Meets have been held in Cumbria for hundreds of years, and were important occasions in the past, when sheep that had wandered from their own grazing area, known as a 'heaf', could be returned to their owners. Each fell area had its own Shepherds' Meets, which were held twice a year – in July for clipping (shearing) time, and in November for tupping (mating). Shepherding can be a solitary occupation and these occasions allowed the shepherds to socialise together and enjoy traditional fare such as Tatie-Pot, a hearty hot-pot made from mutton or lamb, black pudding and 'taties' – potatoes. Shepherds' Meets still occur, and although nowadays they are more in the form of traditional agricultural shows, they are still enjoyable social occasions.

RECIPE

TATIE-POT

1kg/2 lbs lean neck of lamb,
  trimmed and cut into small chunks
1 whole black pudding (about 350g/12oz in weight),
  cut into slices
900g/2 lbs potatoes, peeled and cut into thick slices
2 onions
225g/8oz carrots
1 small turnip (optional)
600ml/1 pint stock
1 bay leaf
Half a teaspoonful chopped dried thyme
Salt and pepper
25g/1oz butter, melted

Pre-heat the oven to 180°C/350°F/Gas Mark 4.

Put the cubed meat and sliced black pudding into a large casserole
dish. Cut the carrots, onions and turnip (if using) into slices, and add
to the casserole. Pour the stock over, add the bay leaf and thyme and
season well with salt and pepper. Arrange the potato slices in an
overlapping layer on top of the vegetables in the casserole. Season
with salt and pepper and brush the potatoes with the melted butter.
Cook the dish with its lid or a piece of foil, and bake in the pre-
heated oven for 2-3 hours, until the potatoes are tender. Remove the
casserole lid or foil and cook for a further 30-45 minutes, to brown
and crisp the potatoes to your liking.

Tatie-Pot is traditionally served with cold pickled red cabbage – see
the recipe on page 27.

RECIPE

WESTMORLAND SWEET PIE

Cumbria is a modern county formed from the old counties of
Cumberland and Westmorland, as well as part of Lancashire. These
old counties are reflected in the names of some of the recipes in
this book, such as this one, Westmorland Sweet Pie. In the past,
mincemeat contained meat as well as dried fruit, hence the name.
A sweet pie made with minced mutton or lamb, dried fruit and
spices was the traditional fare at Christmas time in the past in both
Cumberland and Westmorland.

**BRAMPTON, MARKET PLACE AND ST MARTIN'S CHURCH
c1955** B520001

For the pastry:
350g/12oz plain flour
75g/3oz butter or margarine
75g/3oz lard
A small amount of water,
   to mix
A small amount of milk,
   to glaze

For the pie:
225g/8oz lean minced lamb
675g/1½ lbs mixed dried fruit
   – currants, raisins, sultanas,
   mixed peel
115g/4oz soft brown sugar
4 tablespoonfuls of rum
A good pinch of ground mace
A good pinch of freshly grated
   nutmeg
A good pinch of ground
   cinnamon
Salt and freshly grated black
   pepper

First, make the pastry: rub the butter or margarine and lard into the flour until the mixture resembles fine breadcrumbs. Add just enough water to form a soft dough, and knead the dough lightly until it is smooth and pliable. Leave the dough to rest in a cool place for 30 minutes.

Pre-heat the oven to 200°C/400°F/Gas Mark 6.

Mix the minced lamb with the mixed dried fruit. Add the rum, sugar, mace, nutmeg and cinnamon, season with salt and pepper and mix it all well together. Divide the pastry into two halves, roll out one half on a lightly floured surface and use it to line a greased large, shallow ovenproof pie dish. Put the filling into the pie dish. Roll out the remaining pastry and use it to make a lid for the pie dish, moistening the edges of the pastry and crimping firmly to seal them together. Prick the pastry lid all over with a fork to make small holes for steam to escape during cooking, then brush the pastry lid with a little milk to glaze. Bake in the pre-heated oven for about 30 minutes, until the pastry is crisp and golden.

1858

SEDBURGH, MARKET PLACE 1894 34077

RECIPE

BACON AND APPLE PLATE PIE

This savoury pie is another dish which is traditionally served with pickled red cabbage – see the recipe on page 27. This pie is called a plate pie because it should be made in something fairly flat and wide, such as a sloping-sided pie tin or pie plate with an 18-20 cms (7-8ins) base; alternatively you can use an oven-proof dinner plate 22-24cms (9-10 ins) in diameter.

> 225g/8oz shortcrust pastry
> 1 large cooking apple
> 225g/8oz bacon rashers, de-rinded
> 1 onion, peeled and thinly sliced
> 115g/4oz potatoes, peeled and thinly sliced
> Salt and pepper
> 1 teaspoonful chopped fresh sage
> (or ½ teaspoonful of chopped dried sage)
> 4 teaspoonfuls of light ale

Pre-heat the oven to 200°C/400°F/Gas Mark 6 and place a baking tray in the oven to heat up. Grease the pie tin or plate.

Bring a pan of hot water to the boil, add the potato slices and blanch them in briskly boiling water for 1 minute, then drain well.

Divide the pastry in half. Roll out one half on a lightly floured board and use it to line the greased pie tin. Peel, core and slice the apple, and cut the bacon rashers into quarters. Place a layer each of bacon, sliced onion, apple and blanched potatoes in the pastry-lined pie-plate. Season to taste with salt and pepper and sprinkle over the sage. Spoon the light ale over the filling. Roll out the remaining pastry and use it to make lid for the pie. Cut a couple of slits in the lid to allow steam to escape during cooking, and brush the top with a little milk or beaten egg to glaze. Place the pie on the hot baking tray in the pre-heated oven (this helps the pastry base to cook through properly) and bake for about 50 minutes, until the pastry is crisp and golden and the filling is cooked through.

COCKERMOUTH, MAIN STREET 1906 54992

CUMBERLAND SAUSAGE

Traditional Cumberland Sausage is a specific sort of sausage that originated in Cumberland and was granted Protected Geographical Indication (PGI) status in 2011. Cumberland Sausage has a high meat content and is well-seasoned with spices, particularly pepper, and herbs such as sage and marjoram. It is made in one long length, rather than in individual sausage links as elsewhere in England. Cumberland Sausage is traditionally sold by length, rather than by weight, and is sold rolled up in a flat, circular coil. Another feature of Cumberland Sausage is that it is made of chopped meat, not minced, which gives it a distinctive chunky texture. The best way to cook a Traditional Cumberland Sausage is in a buttered roasting tin, kept in a fairly tight coil. Prick the sausage well all over with a fork and bake for 30 minutes at 180°C/350°F/Gas Mark 4 until well browned all over, turning the coil over once during the cooking time.

RECIPE

CUMBERLAND-STYLE BAKED HAM

1 ham joint, about 4.5kg/10 lbs in weight
Juice of half a lemon
50g/2oz dried breadcrumbs
25g/1oz soft brown sugar
1 teaspoonful made English mustard

Soak the ham overnight in cold water. Place the ham in a large saucepan with the lemon juice, and cover with fresh cold water. Bring to the boil, cover the pan and simmer gently for 3½ hours, replenishing the pan with more boiling water from time to time, and making sure that the pan does not boil dry. When cooked, remove the ham from the pan and reserve 150ml (¼ pint) of the cooking stock. (The rest of the cooking stock should not be discarded, as it can be kept to use as a base for soups.)

Strip off the skin from the ham. With a sharp knife, mark a diamond pattern on the fat left beneath the skin. Mix the breadcrumbs with the sugar and mustard, and spread the mixture all over the ham. Place the ham in a roasting tin, and pour in 150ml (¼ pint) of the ham stock that the ham was boiled in. Cover with foil and bake in the pre-heated oven for about 30 minutes, to finish.

The ham can then be eaten hot or cold, and is delicious served with its traditional accompaniment of Cumberland Sauce – see the recipe on the opposite page.

RECIPE

CUMBERLAND SAUCE

Cumberland Sauce makes a delicious accompaniment to meat, poultry (especially duck), game and sausages. It can be served either hot or cold, although it is traditionally served cold. This makes enough for 4-6 people.

4 large tablespoonfuls good quality redcurrant jelly
4 tablespoonfuls port wine
1 orange
1 lemon
1 heaped teaspoonful English mustard powder
1 heaped teaspoonful ground ginger

Pare the rinds off the orange and lemon very thinly, using a sharp knife or potato peeler. (Reserve the rest of the fruit for later.) Cut the rind as thinly as possible into small strips about 1cm (½ inch) in length. Blanch the strips of peel in a small pan of boiling water for five minutes to remove any bitterness. Drain well in a sieve and keep to one side.

Put the redcurrant jelly and port wine in a saucepan, bring to the boil, then reduce the heat and simmer for 10 minutes whilst the jelly dissolves. Remove from the heat and put the mixture through a sieve to remove any small globules of jelly that remain, then return it to the pan. In a small bowl, blend the mustard powder and ground ginger with the juice of half the lemon to make a smooth paste, then add it to the mixture in the pan, together with the lemon and orange peel and the juice of the whole orange. Combine it well together, then return to the heat, bring to the boil and let it all bubble away for 2-3 minutes to reduce down a little, but not too much – Cumberland Sauce should have a thin consistency, and is not a thick sauce. Either use straight away or leave to cool down to serve cold, if preferred. The sauce can also be stored in a screw-top jar in the fridge to use later, either hot or cold.

RECIPE

HOT RED CABBAGE

This is a traditional hot accompaniment to rich meat such as venison, game, pork and ham.

> 1 red cabbage
> 2 cooking apples
> 1 tablespoonful soft brown sugar
> 1 onion
> 600ml/1 pint water
> 4 tablespoonfuls of red wine
> 4 cloves
> Salt and pepper

Shred the cabbage, and discard the core. Peel, core and slice the apples, and peel and chop the onion. Place the cabbage, apple and onion in a large saucepan with the sugar, salt, pepper, red wine, water and cloves. Bring to the boil, then reduce heat, cover the pan and simmer gently for 2 hours. Strain when cooked, and serve hot as an accompaniment to meat.

KIRKBY LONSDALE, MARKET SQUARE 1908
59539

RECIPE

PICKLED RED CABBAGE

This is served cold, and is the traditional accompaniment to Tatie-Pot (page 17) and Bacon and Apple Plate Pie (page 22). It is also very good served with cold meat. Use jars with screw-top lids lined with plastic, or Kilner jars with glass lids and rubber seals, to make this – tops or lids which are metal alone will corrode.

> 1 red cabbage
> Plenty of cooking salt
> 600ml/1 pint white malt vinegar
> 1 tablespoonful mixed pickling spice
> 25g/1oz sugar
> 1 small raw beetroot, cut into slices (optional)

Remove the tough outer leaves and core from the cabbage, and finely shred the rest of it. Spread the cabbage in a large shallow container like a roasting pan and sprinkle liberally with salt. Cover, and leave to stand overnight. The next day, put the cabbage in a colander and rinse under cold running water to wash off the salt, drain it well then pack it loosely into sterilized large wide-necked jars, to come to 2.5cms (one inch) from the top. A few slices of raw beetroot can also be added on top of the mixture in each jar, as this helps the cabbage maintain a deep red colour.

Put the vinegar, sugar and pickling spices into a large saucepan. Bring to the boil and continue to boil for 10-15 minutes, then remove from the heat, cover and leave for at least 2 hours for the flavour to develop. If you want a stronger flavour let stand for longer, or make up the pickling vinegar the night before, when the cabbage is prepared.

Pour the cooled pickling vinegar over the cabbage in the jars, leaving a 1cm (½ inch) space at the top. Seal the jars tightly with their lids and store in a cool, dark place. Keep for at least 1 week before serving for the flavour to develop, but don't store this too long before using, or the cabbage will lose its delicious crispiness.

LITTLE LANGDALE 1888 20495

RECIPE

CUMBERLAND HERB PUDDING

This savoury pudding was traditionally served as an accompaniment to spring lamb, and includes nettles. The young tender leaves of other wild green plants in the spring, such as dandelion, might also have been included. The young shoots of nettles have been eaten in the spring by country people for centuries, as a source of fresh greens at the time of year known as the 'hungry gap' before other vegetables are ready to eat. Only the tender top sprigs of nettles should be picked and eaten – and the acid which causes the nettles to sting is destroyed by cooking. The children's author Beatrix Potter lived in the Lake District from 1905 until her death in 1943; her first property was Hill Top Farm at Near Sawrey (close to Ambleside), which is now in the care of the National Trust, and after her marriage to Lakeland solicitor William Heelis in 1913 she lived at Castle Cottage on Castle Farm, opposite Hill Top. Beatrix Potter commemorated the local delicacy of Herb Pudding in her book 'The Tale of Johnny Town Mouse' of 1918, when Timmy Willie welcomed Johnny Town Mouse to his home with the words: "You have come at the best of all the year, we will have herb pudding and sit in the sun."

A similar pudding to Herb Pudding was also made in Cumbria in the past using the young green leaves of the Easter Ledge plant, as well as other wild green plants – Easter Ledge ('persicaria bistorta'), also known as Sweet Dock, Common Bistort or Snake Root, is a wild plant with leaves similar to spinach, which grows in the roadside verges and hay meadows of the Lake District. Easter-Ledge Pudding sometimes included oatmeal as well, and was traditionally served at Easter-time.

> 1 tablespoonful of pearl barley
> 450g/1 lb spring cabbage, washed and shredded
> 115g/4oz nettle sprigs, washed
> 2 onions, peeled and finely chopped
> 2 leeks, washed, trimmed and finely chopped
> 25g/1oz butter
> 1 egg
> Salt and pepper

CRUMMOCK WATER, FROM LOWESWATER 1889 22139

Soak the pearl barley overnight in 1 pint of water. The next day, boil it in the same water until it is tender – this will take about 40 minutes. Place the prepared vegetables and nettles in a large, heavy saucepan and add the cooked barley and the water in which it was cooked. Add a little more water if necessary, so that all the ingredients are covered. Bring to the boil and continue boiling quickly until all the vegetables are tender, keeping the lid on the pan, stirring occasionally to make sure that no barley sticks to the base of the pan – this can take between 20-30 minutes, depending on the age and quality of the vegetables. When cooked, drain through a colander, discarding the liquid, and put the vegetables and barley back into the pan. Add the butter and beaten egg, season to taste with salt and pepper, and mix it all together well.

Pre-heat the oven to 180°C/350°F/Gas Mark 4. Turn the mixture into a greased 1.2 litre/2 pint ovenproof dish. Cover with foil and place in the pre-heated oven for 10-15 minutes. Serve hot, turned out of the basin onto a warmed serving dish.

RECIPE

STICKY TOFFEE PUDDING

Sticky Toffee Pudding is one of Britain's great puddings. It consists of a very moist sponge cake, made with finely chopped dates which melt down into the mixture whilst cooking, that is served with a delicious toffee sauce. Although there are rival claims that the pudding may have been invented either in Scotland or Yorkshire, there is a strong Lakeland tradition that Sticky Toffee Pudding originated in Cumbria in the 1960s, when Francis Coulson developed it to serve at his Sharrow Bay Country House Hotel beside Lake Ullswater. Whatever the true origin, Mr Coulson certainly refined the recipe and introduced it to the general public, making it the classic British dessert that it is today. The Cartmel peninsula of southern Cumbria is now the home of The Sticky Toffee Pudding Company, which makes the puddings at its bakery in Flookburgh and sells them at the village shop in nearby Cartmel. Serves 4-6.

For the sponge pudding:
200g/7oz whole dates
(preferably juicy Medjool dates)
1 teaspoonful bicarbonate of
  soda
200ml/8fl oz boiling water
75g/3oz butter, softened
150g/5oz soft brown sugar
2 eggs, beaten
175/6oz self-raising flour

For the sauce:
175g/6oz dark soft brown sugar
50g/2oz butter
300ml/10fl oz double cream
Half a teaspoonful vanilla extract

Pre-heat the oven to 180°C/350°F/Gas Mark 4 and grease and line a loaf tin about 24 x 10cms (9.5 x 4ins) or a baking tin about 20cms (8ins) square, or equivalent.

First, make the sponge pudding. Stone the dates and chop them into quite small pieces, put them in a bowl, add the bicarbonate of soda and pour on the boiling water. Leave to stand for about 20 minutes until they are cool and well-soaked, then mash the soaked dates in the remaining liquid roughly with a fork.

Cream together the butter and soft brown sugar until light and fluffy. Gradually beat in the beaten eggs, a little at a time so the mixture doesn't curdle. Sift in the flour and use a large metal spoon to fold it into the mixture. Gently stir the mashed dates and any remaining liquid into the pudding batter, which will be soft and thick, and mix until smooth. Pour the mixture into the prepared tin, and bake in the pre-heated oven for about 45 minutes, until the pudding is risen and firm. Allow to stand and settle in the tin for 10 minutes whilst you make the toffee sauce.

To make the sauce: put the sugar and butter for the sauce into a medium saucepan with half the cream and the vanilla essence and bring to the boil over a medium heat, stirring all the time, until the sugar has completely dissolved. Then let the mixture bubble away for 5 minutes until it is a rich toffee colour and has thickened slightly, stirring continually to ensure the sauce doesn't burn. Take the pan off the heat and allow the mixture to cool for a few minutes, then beat in the rest of the cream.

Loosen the pudding well from the sides of the tin with a small palette knife before turning it out onto a plate. Serve the pudding cut into thick slabs with a generous amount of the toffee sauce poured over each helping, perhaps accompanied by cream, custard or ice-cream.

Cook's tip: to make the pudding even stickier, you can pour the sauce over it and then leave it to stand for a day or two, coated in the sauce. To do this, pour about half the sauce into an ovenproof serving dish. Sit the turned-out pudding on the sauce, and then pour the rest of the sauce over it. Cover the dish loosely with foil, and leave the pudding to stand in a cool place until needed, when it can be re-heated in the oven (180C°/350°F/Gas Mark 4), still covered in foil, until the sauce is bubbling.

RECIPE

CONISTON PUDDING

For the pastry:
175g/6oz plain flour
75g/3oz butter or margarine
25g/1oz caster sugar
1 egg

For the filling:
25g/1oz caster sugar
1 egg
A pinch of freshly grated
  nutmeg
75ml/2.5fl oz hot milk, mixed
  with 75ml/2.5fl oz single cream
25g/1oz raisins
25g/1oz currants
15g/ ½ oz chopped candied
  peel

Rub the butter into the flour until the mixture resembles fine breadcrumbs. Stir in the sugar, then mix in the egg to form a soft dough. Leave to rest for 30 minutes, then roll out the dough and line a greased flan or pie dish about 20cms (8ins) in diameter.

Pre-heat the oven to 180°C/350°F/Gas Mark 4 and place a baking sheet in the oven to heat up whilst you prepare the filling. Beat the egg and add the sugar and nutmeg. Add the hot milk and cream mixture, the raisins, currants and candied peel, and mix well. Pour the mixture into the pastry case, place the dish on the hot baking sheet in the oven (this helps the pastry base to cook through) and bake for about 50 minutes, until the pastry is cooked and the filling is lightly set and golden brown.

CONISTON, THE LAKE FROM BEACON'S CRAG 1929 82789

RECIPE

DAMSON FOOL

Cumbria is famous for its damsons, especially those grown in the Lyth valley south of Windermere. These are known as Witherslack damsons, after the village of that name, and are large, juicy and much sweeter than damsons grown elsewhere in the country. Serves 6.

900g/2 lbs damsons
225g/8oz caster sugar
600ml/1 pint milk
300ml/ ½ pint double cream
4 egg yolks
1 tablespoonful lemon juice
A little extra double cream for decoration

Gently stew the damsons with the sugar and a very small amount of water in a saucepan over a very low heat until they are soft and tender. Push the fruit through a sieve to remove the skins and stones, then allow the fruit purée to cool.

Mix the milk and cream together and heat in a saucepan to boiling point. Whisk the egg yolks in a separate bowl, then pour a little of the boiling milk mixture onto the egg yolks and continue whisking. Pour the egg mixture into the saucepan with the milk, and cook over a low heat until the mixture thickens to form a custard, stirring continually. When the mixture has thickened, remove from the heat and allow it to cool. Mix the damson purée with the custard and stir in the lemon juice. Pour the mixture into either one large serving dish or individual glass dishes. Keep in the fridge until ready to serve, decorated with a little whipped cream.

RECIPE

WESTMORLAND THREE DECKER

This delicious three-layered fruit pie can be made with either plums or the famous Witherslack damsons from the Lyth valley south of Windermere. Alternatively, use 450g/1 lb of apples, peeled, cored and sliced, to make a hearty apple pie, or equal quantities of sliced apples and blackberries. The middle layer of pastry cooks down to thicken the fruit juices.

> 350g/12oz plain flour
> A pinch of salt
> 175g/6oz butter or margarine
> A little cold water
> 450g/1 lb plums or large damsons, cut in half
>   and their stones removed
> 50g/2oz caster sugar (or more, to taste)
> A little milk to glaze
> 1 tablespoonful extra sugar to finish

Sift the flour and salt into a bowl, then rub in the butter or margarine until the mixture resembles fine breadcrumbs. Add enough cold water to mix it all into a soft dough, knead lightly and leave to rest in a cool place for 30 minutes.

Pre-heat the oven to 190°C/375°F/Gas Mark 5. Divide the dough into three equal pieces. Roll out one piece on a lightly-floured surface and use it to line a greased pie plate or tin. Place half the fruit in the pie dish and sprinkle half the sugar over it. Roll out the second piece of dough and place it over the fruit. Put the remaining fruit on top, and sprinkle with the remaining sugar. Roll out the last piece of dough and place it on top. Brush the top with a little milk to glaze and sprinkle it with the extra sugar. Bake in the pre-heated oven for 20 minutes, then reduce the oven temperature to 180°C/350°F/Gas Mark 5 and bake for a further 30 minutes or so, until the pastry is crisp and golden and the fruit filling is cooked. Serve with cream or custard, and a little extra sugar if needed.

AMBLESIDE, BRIDGE HOUSE 1912 64306
The most iconic building of Ambleside is the tiny one-up, one-down
Bridge House, which was constructed on a bridge over the Stock Beck
to escape land tax. It is now a National Trust shop, but was originally
built in 1723 as an apple-store for the now-demolished Ambleside Hall.

RECIPE

CUMBERLAND APPLE PUDDING

75g/3oz self-raising flour
75g/3oz fresh breadcrumbs
75g/3oz shredded suet
75g/3oz soft brown sugar
2 large eggs, beaten
1 large cooking apple
Grated rind of 1 lemon
A pinch of freshly grated nutmeg
1 tablespoonful golden syrup, warmed
4-6 tablespoonfuls milk
A pinch of salt

Grease a 1.2 litre (2 pint) pudding basin. Mix together the flour, breadcrumbs, suet, sugar, nutmeg, lemon rind and salt. Peel, core and finely chop the apple, then stir it into the flour mixture with the warmed syrup and beaten eggs, adding just enough milk to form a soft dough. Mix it all thoroughly, then turn the mixture into the greased pudding basin. Cover the top of the basin with pleated greaseproof paper (to allow room for rising), and then a piece of pleated foil and tie down firmly with string. Place the basin in a large saucepan of boiling water, cover the pan with its lid, and steam for about 1½ hours. Top up the pan with more boiling water from time to time, so the pan doesn't boil dry. When cooked, turn out the pudding onto a serving dish and serve piping hot, with custard or cream.

One of England's most eccentric events takes place at Egremont, near Whitehaven, every September – the World Gurning Championship. Gurning is the art of making grotesque faces, and the winner of this event is the person who receives the most applause from the audience for pulling a grotesque expression whilst looking through a horse's collar. The Gurning Championships take place during the Egremont Crab Apple Fair, which dates back to 1267 when it was first held to celebrate the local lord of the manor wheeling a cart of crab apples through the village to distribute to the poor. Crab apples are sour and bitter, and it may be that the gurning competition originated from the faces the village people made as they bit into the sharp-tasting apples.

Flavours of ...
CUMBRIA
PUDDINGS, PIES & DESSERTS

39

RECIPE

CLIPPING-DAY PUDDING

Early summer is when sheep are sheared of their winter wool. In the past, clipping off the fleeces was done with hand shears, an exceedingly tiring job, but electric shears are used nowadays. Clipping-Day Pudding was a traditional dish to serve at shearing time, and was either taken out to the clippers by the farmer's wife or served at clipping-time suppers in the evenings when the day's work was done – these were jolly events with lots of singing and dancing, but the tradition of clipping-time suppers seems to have died out around the mid 20th century, when hand clippers ceased to be used. Clipping-Day Pudding is like a spicy, fruity rice pudding which was traditionally enriched with bone marrow; however, butter may be more to modern tastes, so that is used here instead. This makes a lovely hot pudding served with a little cream, but it was traditionally eaten cold as well, cut into wedges and spread with either butter or bone marrow. Serves 4-6.

115g/4oz pudding rice
600ml/1 pint milk
75g/3oz sugar
1 teaspoonful ground cinnamon
25g/1oz butter
115g/4oz currants
115g/4oz raisins
1 egg, beaten
A pinch of salt

Put 300ml/½ pint water in a small pan, lightly salt it and bring to the boil. Add the pudding rice, stir well so it doesn't stick to the bottom, and boil for 2-3 minutes. Drain the blanched rice. Put the milk in a large pan, add the rice, sugar and cinnamon, mix well and gently bring it to the boil, stirring occasionally. Reduce the heat to a simmer and cook for about 30 minutes, stirring occasionally, until the rice is soft and tender. Pre-heat the oven to 180°C/350°F/Gas Mark 4 and grease a 1.2 litre/2 pint ovenproof dish. When the rice is tender, remove the pan from the heat and add the butter, stirring until it is completely melted, then stir in the currants and raisins and a pinch of salt. Leave to cool for a few minutes, then mix in the beaten egg. Turn the mixture into the prepared dish and bake in the pre-heated oven for about 20 minutes, until the pudding is golden on top and just set.

**CALDBECK
SHEEP SHEARING
c1955** C567031

KENDAL, THE FLEECE INN AND CLARENCE WEBB'S SHOP 1914 67372

One of the Cumbrian towns whose wealth was won from the wool of sheep in the past was Kendal – the 'Auld Grey Town' beside the River Kent that was famous for its wool and textile industries for centuries. Its motto is 'Pannis mihi Panis', which means 'wool is my bread'. A reminder of the historic importance of wool to the town is the name of Ye Olde Fleece Inn in Highgate, the oldest surviving inn still in business in Kendal. To the left of the Fleece Inn in this photograph of 1914 are the premises of Clarence Webb, seed merchant, grower and nurseryman. Clarence Webb was a noted horticulturist who was very interested in producing improved varieties of flowers and vegetables. One of his greatest successes was the development of a variety of lettuce called 'Webb's Wonderful Lettuce', which he registered in 1890; it is now one of the most popular lettuce varieties in the UK. Kendal is also famous for Kendal Mint Cake, a confectionary combination of sugar, glucose and peppermint and is a favourite with walkers, athletes and mountaineers as it gives energy quickly.

RECIPE

KENDAL WIGS

There are several recipes from Cumbria for these small buns, known variously as Wigs, Wiggs or Whigs. This is from Kendal, but there is another version from Hawkshead which includes caraway seeds, a popular flavouring for biscuits and cakes in the past.

450g/1 lb plain flour
50g/2oz lard
50g/2oz soft brown sugar
25g/1oz fresh yeast, or 3 teaspoonfuls quick-acting
  dried yeast
300ml/ ½ pint warm water
A pinch of salt
25g/1oz currants

Dissolve the sugar in the warm water, add the yeast, then leave it for about ten minutes, until it becomes frothy. Rub the lard into the flour and add a pinch of salt. When the yeast mixture is ready, pour it into the dry ingredients and mix it all to form a soft dough, adding a little milk if necessary. Knead the dough for about ten minutes, until it is smooth and elastic, then knead the currants into the dough.

Leave the dough to rise in a warm place, in a bowl covered with a clean cloth or inside a greased polythene bag, until it has doubled in size. Divide the dough into about 20 small pieces and shape them into buns. Place the buns on greased baking sheets, well spaced out, and leave to rise again in a warm place for about 1 hour.

Pre-heat the oven to 200°C/400°F/Gas Mark 6, then bake the buns for about 15 minutes, and serve warm. These are very good spread with Cumberland Rum Butter – see the recipe on page 53.

RECIPE

CUMBERLAND LEMON CAKE

In former centuries the port of Whitehaven was one of the leading ports in the country trading with the West Indies, importing rum, ginger, treacle, exotic fruit, brown sugar and spices. All these items figure prominently in traditional fare from the area.

175g/6oz butter or margarine, softened
150g/5oz caster sugar
2 eggs, beaten
225g/8oz self-raising flour
2 tablespoonfuls lemon juice
Finely-grated rind of 1 lemon
50g/2oz candied lemon peel, finely chopped
1 tablespoonful milk
Icing sugar, to finish

Pre-heat the oven to 180°C/350°F/Gas Mark 4. Grease and line a cake tin about 18-20cms (7-8ins) in diameter. Cream the butter or margarine and sugar together until light and fluffy. Gradually mix in the beaten eggs, a little at a time, adding 1 tablespoonful of the flour at the same time to prevent the mixture curdling. Mix thoroughly, then fold in the rest of the flour with a large metal spoon. Add the lemon juice, the finely grated lemon rind and the chopped candied lemon peel. Mix well, and only add the tablespoonful of milk if the mixture seems too stiff – you should end up with a firm, dropping consistency. Pour the mixture into the prepared cake tin and bake in the centre of the pre-heated oven for about 1 hour, until firm and pale brown. Check that the cake is cooked by inserting a small metal skewer into the centre, which will come out clean when the cake is ready. If necessary, continue cooking for up to a further 30 minutes. Leave to cool in the tin for 15 minutes before removing and leaving to cool completely on a wire rack. Sift icing sugar across the top before serving.

This is very good as it is, but it can also be made into a lemon sandwich-style cake if you cut it across into two rounds, spread one side with lemon curd, and then sandwich the two rounds back together.

RECITE

RECIPE

CUMBERLAND RUM NICKIES

There are several versions of Rum Nickies. This recipe is for small individual Nickies which are rather like mince pies.

<u>For the pastry:</u>
225g/8oz plain flour
115g/4oz butter or
  margarine
A pinch of salt
A little cold water
A little milk to glaze

<u>For the filling:</u>
25g/1oz butter or margarine
115g/4oz currants
25g/1oz brown sugar
Half a teaspoonful freshly
  grated nutmeg
1 tablespoonful rum

First make the filling mixture. Melt the butter in a large saucepan, and add the rum and nutmeg. Add the sugar and currants and leave to steep for 1 hour.

Whilst the filling is steeping, make a pastry dough. Sift the flour and salt into a bowl and rub in the butter or margarine until the mixture resembles fine breadcrumbs. Add just enough cold water to mix it to a soft dough. Knead lightly until the dough is smooth and elastic, then leave to rest in a cool place for 30 minutes.

Pre-heat the oven to 200°C/400°F/Gas Mark 6. Roll out the pastry on a lightly floured surface and cut it into rounds about 8cms (3ins) in diameter. Place a spoonful of the filling mixture in the middle of half the pastry circles, and brush the edges with a little water. Cover each filled circle with one of the remaining pastry circles, and pinch the edges together well to seal. Use a sharp knife to cut a couple of slits, or nicks, across the top of each Nickie, to allow steam to escape whilst cooking, and brush with milk to glaze. Place the Nickies on a greased baking sheet and bake in the pre-heated oven for about 12-15 minutes, until the pastry is crisp and golden brown.

RECIPE

BORROWDALE TEABREAD

Many local recipes in Cumbria for various forms of cakes and biscuits originated in the 19th century, when they were developed to serve to the tourists who were starting to visit the region. You will need to soak the dried fruit in hot, milkless tea overnight before making it, which makes the fruit lovely and juicy, resulting in a deliciously moist and tasty teabread.

275g/10oz mixed dried fruit – sultanas, raisins, currants
115g/4oz soft light brown sugar
275ml/ ½ pint hot milkless tea (made with one tea bag)
25g/1oz butter, melted
1 egg, beaten
225g/8oz self-raising wholemeal flour

Put the dried fruit in a bowl and add the hot, milkless tea. Cover the bowl and leave the fruit to soak overnight.

Pre-heat the oven to 180°C/350°F/Gas Mark 4 (slightly less for a fan oven). Grease and line a 900g/2lb loaf tin, about 22 x 12cms (8½ x 4½ ins) or equivalent.

Put the soaked dried fruit and the remaining soaking liquid into a large mixing bowl. Stir in the flour, sugar, and melted butter and beat it all together well, then add the beaten egg and mix in well. Pour the mixture into the prepared loaf tin. Bake just below the centre of the pre-heated oven for about 45 minutes, until the cake is well risen and golden, and firm to the touch – check it towards the end of the cooking time, and bake for a little longer if it looks like it can take it. Leave in the tin for 15 minutes to settle before turning out.

This can be eaten either warm or cold, cut into thin slices and spread with butter.

BORROWDALE, THE BOWDER STONE c1880 B146301

Borrowdale is one of the wildest valleys of Lakeland. Early tourists were 'horrified' at the expanses of naked rock and impending mountains of places like Borrowdale, and feared to travel far into the dale, until poets like William Wordsworth (1770-1850) popularized the 'picturesque' mountain scenery. The Bowder Stone near Grange in Borrowdale is a 2,000-ton boulder which was transported there by Ice Age glaciers, and has been a source of tourist wonder for centuries. The scene looks very different today from how it appears in this view from the 1880s, as the stone is now surrounded by trees, but there is still a wooden staircase to reach the top.

BUTTERMERE, HIGH STILE 1889 22065

RECIPE

BUTTERMERE BISCUITS

One theory about the origin of the name of Buttermere in the western Lake District is that it means 'the lake by the dairy pastures', and using butter in these fruited biscuits makes them especially delicious. This should make about 15 biscuits.

> 225g/8oz plain flour
> Half a teaspoonful baking powder
> A pinch of salt
> 50g/2oz currants
> 115g/4oz butter
> 115g/4oz caster sugar
> Grated rind of 1 lemon
> 1 large egg, beaten
> A little milk and granulated sugar, to finish

Pre-heat the oven to 180°C/350°F/Gas Mark 4 (slightly less for a fan oven), and grease two baking sheets. Sift the flour into a bowl with the baking powder and salt. Rub in the butter, stir in the currants, sugar and lemon rind then use a round-bladed knife to mix the beaten egg into the mixture and gather it into your hand to form a stiff dough. Roll it out on a lightly floured surface to 7mm (¼ inch) thick. Cut out rounds with a biscuit cutter 75mm (3ins) in diameter. Brush the rounds with milk and scatter a little granulated sugar on top. Place them on the baking sheets, spaced well apart, and bake in the pre-heated oven for 15-20 minutes, until they are firm and golden brown.

RECIPE

GRASMERE GINGERBREAD

The Cumbrian village of Grasmere is famous for its gingerbread, but there are a number of versions associated with it. A particularly famous version of Grasmere Gingerbread was made by Sarah Nelson, who came to Grasmere from Lancashire in the 1850s and set up business there. Her gingerbread is still made and sold from a small shop in the village, but her own particular recipe is a closely-guarded secret. Other variations from the area are a thin, crisp gingerbread that is rather like a ginger shortbread, and the thicker version given here, which includes eggs and makes a crumbly gingerbread that is rather different from the soft cake style made elsewhere in the country. This should make 9-12 portions, depending on how large you want them.

225g/8oz self-raising flour
1-2 teaspoonfuls ground ginger, according to taste
¼ teaspoonful salt
75g/3oz granulated sugar
115g/4oz butter or margarine
1 dessertspoonful golden syrup
2 eggs, separated
75g/3oz finely chopped mixed peel (optional)
2 extra tablespoonfuls granulated sugar for the topping

Pre-heat the oven to 170°C/325°F/Gas Mark 3. Grease a baking tin about 20cms (8ins) square or equivalent. Sift the flour and ground ginger into a bowl and mix in the salt and sugar. Add the chopped peel, if using. Melt the butter or margarine in a pan with the golden syrup over a low heat until it is dissolved. Remove the pan from the heat and leave to cool for five minutes, then stir in the two beaten egg yolks. Pour into the dry ingredients and mix it all well together, to form quite a stiff paste. Press all the mixture into the prepared tin and level the surface. Brush the top liberally with egg white, and sprinkle the extra sugar all over. Bake in the pre-heated oven for about 30 minutes until firm and lightly browned, giving the tin a quarter turn half way through this baking time to cook the cake evenly. Leave in the tin to cool down for about 15 minutes before cutting into individual portions, then leave to cool in the tin completely before taking them out.

GRASMERE, THE CHURCH OF ST OSWALD AND THE RECTORY 1929
82835

Gingerbread features in the picturesque Rushbearing Festival that takes place in Grasmere every year on the nearest Saturday to 5th August, the feast day of St Oswald, to whom Grasmere's atmospheric parish church is dedicated. The festival commemorates a custom that dates back to the days when the earthen floors of churches were strewn with rushes or straw to make them softer underfoot; this covering was renewed before major festivals and, as at Grasmere, before the church's dedication day. Although the floor of St Oswald's Church at Grasmere has been flagged since 1841, the ceremony still continues. A procession passes through the village behind a large cross made of rushes and flowers, accompanied by a band, clergy and children carrying rushes and decorations for the church. After the procession and a special service in the church, the children who have carried the rushes are traditionally given a piece of Grasmere Gingerbread.

The ancient custom of Rushbearing also takes place at Ambleside, Warcop, Great Musgrave and Urswick, where wild rushes and flowers are similarly paraded round the village in procession before being taken to the local church.

RECIPE

OATCAKES

Oatcakes were basic daily food in much of the north of England in the past, where oatmeal formed a staple part of many people's diet because the climate and terrain favoured the cultivation of oats rather than other cereals. Oatcakes are delicious eaten with cheese, or spread with jam, marmalade or Cumberland rum butter – see the recipe on the opposite page.

> 115g/4oz plain flour
> 115g/4oz rolled oats
> 25g/1oz caster sugar
> 50g/2oz butter or margarine
> 25g/1oz lard
> A pinch of salt
> Half a teaspoonful bicarbonate of soda
> 1 tablespoonful water
> A little milk

Pre-heat the oven to 190°C/375°F/Gas Mark 5 and grease a baking sheet.

Sieve the flour into a bowl, and add the rolled oats, sugar and salt. Melt the butter or margarine and lard with the bicarbonate of soda and water in a saucepan, then add to the dry ingredients and mix well, adding just enough milk to form the mixture into a firm dough.

Roll out the dough on a lightly floured surface to about 5mm (¼ inch) thick. Cut out into small circles with a biscuit cutter. Place on the greased baking sheet, well spaced out, and bake in the pre-heated oven for about 15 minutes, until the oatcakes are golden brown.

RECIPE

CUMBERLAND RUM BUTTER

Cumberland rum butter is a delicious regional speciality of butter flavoured with rum, sugar and spices. It was traditionally made by an expectant mother three months before her baby was due. She would press it into a traditional rum butter bowl and put it by until her baby was born, when it would be served on oatcakes to visitors who came to see the new arrival and celebrate the birth. It became the custom in some parts of Cumbria for well-wishers to place coins in the empty bowl when all the rum butter had been consumed, especially at Christening parties, to ensure the newborn child would have a long and prosperous life. Nowadays, rum butter is delicious eaten with scones or steamed puddings, and is especially good with mince pies and Christmas pudding.

  225g/8oz unsalted butter, softened to room temperature
  350g/12oz soft brown sugar
  125ml/4 fl oz dark rum
  A good pinch of ground cinnamon
  A good pinch of ground nutmeg

Beat the butter in a bowl until it is soft and creamy. Beat in the sugar until it is thoroughly blended. Gradually add the rum, beating well after each addition. Add cinnamon and nutmeg to taste, and put the mixture into a small pot or jar. Cover, and store in the refrigerator, and chill well before serving. This will keep well in the refrigerator for several weeks.

FRANCIS FRITH

PIONEER VICTORIAN PHOTOGRAPHER

Francis Frith, founder of the world-famous photographic archive, was a complex and multi-talented man. A devout Quaker and a highly successful Victorian businessman, he was philosophical by nature and pioneering in outlook. By 1855 he had already established a wholesale grocery business in Liverpool, and sold it for the astonishing sum of £200,000, which is the equivalent today of over £15,000,000. Now in his thirties, and captivated by the new science of photography, Frith set out on a series of pioneering journeys up the Nile and to the Near East.

INTRIGUE AND EXPLORATION

He was the first photographer to venture beyond the sixth cataract of the Nile. Africa was still the mysterious 'Dark Continent', and Stanley and Livingstone's historic meeting was a decade into the future. The conditions for picture taking confound belief. He laboured for hours in his wicker dark-room in the sweltering heat of the desert, while the volatile chemicals fizzed dangerously in their trays. Back in London he exhibited his photographs and was 'rapturously cheered' by members of the Royal Society. His reputation as a photographer was made overnight.

VENTURE OF A LIFE-TIME

By the 1870s the railways had threaded their way across the country, and Bank Holidays and half-day Saturdays had been made obligatory by Act of Parliament. All of a sudden the working man and his family were able to enjoy days out, take holidays, and see a little more of the world.

With typical business acumen, Francis Frith foresaw that these new tourists would enjoy having souvenirs to commemorate their days out. For the next thirty years he travelled the country by train and by pony and trap, producing fine photographs of seaside resorts and beauty spots that were keenly bought by millions of Victorians. These prints were painstakingly pasted into family albums and pored over during the dark nights of winter, rekindling precious memories of summer excursions. Frith's studio was soon supplying retail shops all over the country, and by 1890 F Frith & Co had become the greatest specialist photographic publishing company in the world, with over 2,000 sales outlets, and pioneered the picture postcard.

FRANCIS FRITH'S LEGACY

Francis Frith had died in 1898 at his villa in Cannes, his great project still growing. By 1970 the archive he created contained over a third of a million pictures showing 7,000 British towns and villages.

Frith's legacy to us today is of immense significance and value, for the magnificent archive of evocative photographs he created provides a unique record of change in the cities, towns and villages throughout Britain over a century and more. Frith and his fellow studio photographers revisited locations many times down the years to update their views, compiling for us an enthralling and colourful pageant of British life and character.

We are fortunate that Frith was dedicated to recording the minutiae of everyday life. For it is this sheer wealth of visual data, the painstaking chronicle of changes in dress, transport, street layouts, buildings, housing and landscape that captivates us so much today, offering us a powerful link with the past and with the lives of our ancestors.

Computers have now made it possible for Frith's many thousands of images to be accessed almost instantly. The archive offers every one of us an opportunity to examine the places where we and our families have lived and worked down the years. Its images, depicting our shared past, are now bringing pleasure and enlightenment to millions around the world a century and more after his death.

For further information visit: www.francisfrith.com

INTERIOR DECORATION

Frith's photographs can be seen framed and as giant wall murals in thousands of pubs, restaurants, hotels, banks, retail stores and other public buildings throughout Britain. These provide interesting and attractive décor, generating strong local interest and acting as a powerful reminder of gentler days in our increasingly busy and frenetic world.

FRITH PRODUCTS

All Frith photographs are available as prints and posters in a variety of different sizes and styles. In the UK we also offer a range of other gift and stationery products illustrated with Frith photographs, although many of these are not available for delivery outside the UK – see our web site for more information on the products available for delivery in your country.

THE INTERNET

Over 100,000 photographs of Britain can be viewed and purchased on the Frith web site. The web site also includes memories and reminiscences contributed by our customers, who have personal knowledge of localities and of the people and properties depicted in Frith photographs. If you wish to learn more about a specific town or village you may find these reminiscences fascinating to browse. Why not add your own comments if you think they would be of interest to others? See **www.francisfrith.com**

PLEASE HELP US BRING FRITH'S PHOTOGRAPHS TO LIFE

Our authors do their best to recount the history of the places they write about. They give insights into how particular towns and villages developed, they describe the architecture of streets and buildings, and they discuss the lives of famous people who lived there. But however knowledgeable our authors are, the story they tell is necessarily incomplete.

Frith's photographs are so much more than plain historical documents. They are living proofs of the flow of human life down the generations. They show real people at real moments in history; and each of those people is the son or daughter of someone, the brother or sister, aunt or uncle, grandfather or grandmother of someone else. All of them lived, worked and played in the streets depicted in Frith's photographs.

We would be grateful if you would give us your insights into the places shown in our photographs: the streets and buildings, the shops, businesses and industries. Post your memories of life in those streets on the Frith website: what it was like growing up there, who ran the local shop and what shopping was like years ago; if your workplace is shown tell us about your working day and what the building is used for now. Read other visitors' memories and reconnect with your shared local history and heritage. With your help more and more Frith photographs can be brought to life, and vital memories preserved for posterity, and for the benefit of historians in the future.

Wherever possible, we will try to include some of your comments in future editions of our books. Moreover, if you spot errors in dates, titles or other facts, please let us know, because our archive records are not always completely accurate—they rely on 140 years of human endeavour and hand-compiled records. You can email us using the contact form on the website.

Thank you!

For further information, trade, or author enquiries
please contact us at the address below:

**The Francis Frith Collection, Oakley Business Park,
Wylye Road, Dinton, Wiltshire SP3 5EU England.**
Tel: +44 (0)1722 716 376 Fax: +44 (0)1722 716 881
e-mail: sales@francisfrith.co.uk **www.francisfrith.com**